YOU KNOW THEY'RE
MADE FOR EACH OTHER
WHEN...

$7-

3/2022

Written By Herbert I. Kavet

Designed and Illustrated By Martin Riskin

Copyright © 1985 by Ivory Tower Publishing Company, Inc.
All Rights Reserved

Published simultaneously in Canada by Marka Canada, Toronto, Ontario

Distributed in the United Kingdom by Azlon London LTD, London SW11 3UP

Distributed in South Africa by Confectomatic Machines (Pty) LTD, Johannesburg 2000

Manufactured in the United States of America

First Printing May 1985

IVORY TOWER PUBLISHING COMPANY, INC.
125 Walnut Street, Watertown, MA 02172   TEL: (617) 923-1111   TELEX: 697-1455 ITAP

YOU KNOW THEY'RE
MADE FOR EACH OTHER
WHEN...

They are willing to share domestic chores.

YOU KNOW THEY'RE
MADE FOR EACH OTHER
WHEN...

They are happy to consolidate their paychecks.

YOU KNOW THEY'RE
MADE FOR EACH OTHER
WHEN...

Their furniture mixes easily together.

YOU KNOW THEY'RE
MADE FOR EACH OTHER
WHEN...

They always agree on necessities.

YOU KNOW THEY'RE
MADE FOR EACH OTHER
WHEN...

Neither would have a problem
living near their families.

YOU KNOW THEY'RE
MADE FOR EACH OTHER
—WHEN...—

They have come to an agreement
on parking their cars.

YOU KNOW THEY'RE
MADE FOR EACH OTHER
WHEN...

Thank God, they've been taught to share.

YOU KNOW THEY'RE
MADE FOR EACH OTHER
WHEN...

They come from kindred family backgrounds.

YOU KNOW THEY'RE
MADE FOR EACH OTHER
WHEN...

Even the aunts approve of the union.

YOU KNOW THEY'RE
MADE FOR EACH OTHER
——WHEN...——

Both want the same kind of wedding.

YOU KNOW THEY'RE
MADE FOR EACH OTHER
WHEN...

They enjoy the same sports.

YOU KNOW THEY'RE
MADE FOR EACH OTHER
WHEN...

Their careers compliment each other.

YOU KNOW THEY'RE
MADE FOR EACH OTHER
WHEN...

They respect each other's intellectual pursuits.

YOU KNOW THEY'RE
MADE FOR EACH OTHER
WHEN...

They love visiting in laws.

YOU KNOW THEY'RE
MADE FOR EACH OTHER
WHEN...

Their religious backgrounds are reconcilable.

YOU KNOW THEY'RE
MADE FOR EACH OTHER
WHEN...

Each remembers the other's clothes size.

YOU KNOW THEY'RE
MADE FOR EACH OTHER
WHEN...

**At least one of them understands
the formalities of etiquette.**

YOU KNOW THEY'RE
MADE FOR EACH OTHER
WHEN...

They tolerate each other's friends.

YOU KNOW THEY'RE
MADE FOR EACH OTHER
WHEN...

They are both pleasant in the morning.

YOU KNOW THEY'RE
MADE FOR EACH OTHER
WHEN...

Neither wins a prize for neatness.

YOU KNOW THEY'RE
MADE FOR EACH OTHER
WHEN...

Both have such interesting jobs.

YOU KNOW THEY'RE
MADE FOR EACH OTHER
WHEN...

One of them always remembers birthdays.

YOU KNOW THEY'RE
MADE FOR EACH OTHER
WHEN...

Sisters - and brothers - in - law will always be welcome

YOU KNOW THEY'RE
MADE FOR EACH OTHER
WHEN...

They agree on honeymoon spots.

YOU KNOW THEY'RE
MADE FOR EACH OTHER
WHEN...

Neither has any repulsive personal habits.

YOU KNOW THEY'RE
MADE FOR EACH OTHER
WHEN...

They are never upset by unusual family customs.

YOU KNOW THEY'RE
MADE FOR EACH OTHER
WHEN...

They understand each other's diets.

YOU KNOW THEY'RE
MADE FOR EACH OTHER
WHEN...

They are always respectful of each other's feelings.

YOU KNOW THEY'RE
MADE FOR EACH OTHER
——WHEN...——

They agree on TV programs.

YOU KNOW THEY'RE
MADE FOR EACH OTHER
WHEN...

They adore each other's pets.

YOU KNOW THEY'RE
MADE FOR EACH OTHER
WHEN...

They support the same causes.

YOU KNOW THEY'RE
MADE FOR EACH OTHER
WHEN...

They are interested in each other's hobbies.

YOU KNOW THEY'RE
MADE FOR EACH OTHER
WHEN...

Neither can cook.

YOU KNOW THEY'RE
MADE FOR EACH OTHER
WHEN...

At least they like the same kind of food.

YOU KNOW THEY'RE
MADE FOR EACH OTHER
———— WHEN... ————

A person who shall remain nameless
once cleaned an oven.

YOU KNOW THEY'RE
MADE FOR EACH OTHER
WHEN...

They adore children.

YOU KNOW THEY'RE
MADE FOR EACH OTHER
—WHEN...—

Both respect each other's space.

YOU KNOW THEY'RE
MADE FOR EACH OTHER
WHEN...

They always can judge each other's moods.

YOU KNOW THEY'RE
MADE FOR EACH OTHER
WHEN...

They know the best ways to relax each other.

YOU KNOW THEY'RE
MADE FOR EACH OTHER
—WHEN...—

Both enjoy the same kind of music.

YOU KNOW THEY'RE
MADE FOR EACH OTHER
WHEN...

One of them knows how to keep plants alive.

YOU KNOW THEY'RE
MADE FOR EACH OTHER
—WHEN...—

They are emotionally compatible.

YOU KNOW THEY'RE
MADE FOR EACH OTHER
WHEN...

One party whose name will remain secret
is finally ready to give up their Teddy Bear.